W9-DFD-972

WITHDRAWN

Journey to Freedom®

SLAVERY:
THE STRUGGLE FOR FREEDOM

BY JAMES MEADOWS

"TO BE A SLAVE. TO BE OWNED BY ANOTHER PERSON, AS A CAR, HOUSE, OR TABLE IS OWNED. TO LIVE AS A PIECE OF PROPERTY THAT COULD BE SOLD—A CHILD SOLD FROM ITS MOTHER, A WIFE FROM HER HUSBAND. TO BE CONSIDERED NOT HUMAN, BUT A THING THAT PLOWED THE FIELDS, CUT THE WOOD, COOKED THE FOOD, NURSED ANOTHER'S CHILD; A THING WHOSE SOLE FUNCTION WAS DETERMINED BY THE ONE WHO OWNED YOU.

"TO BE A SLAVE. TO KNOW DESPITE THE SUFFERING AND DEPRIVATION, THAT YOU WERE HUMAN, MORE HUMAN THAN HE WHO SAID YOU WERE NOT HUMAN. TO KNOW JOY, LAUGHTER, SORROW, AND TEARS AND YET BE CONSIDERED ONLY THE EQUAL OF A TABLE. TO BE A SLAVE WAS TO BE A HUMAN BEING UNDER CONDITIONS IN WHICH THAT HUMANITY WAS DENIED. THEY WERE NOT SLAVES. THEY WERE PEOPLE. THEIR CONDITION WAS SLAVERY."

 JULIUS LESTER

Cover and page 4 caption:
A slave family working in
a Georgia cotton field
around 1860

Content Consultant:
Kira Duke, Education
Coordinator, National Civil
Rights Museum

Published in the United States of America by The Child's World®
1980 Lookout Drive, Mankato, MN 56003-1705
800-599-READ • www.childsworld.com

ACKNOWLEDGEMENTS

The Child's World®: Mary Berendes, Publishing Director

The Design Lab: Kathleen Petelinsek, Design; Gregory Lindholm, Page Production

Red Line Editorial: Erika Wittekind, Editorial Direction

PHOTOS

Cover and page 4: American School/Getty Images

Interior: AP Images, 13, 15, 24; Brady National Photographic Art Gallery/Library of Congress,
25; Charles T. Webber/Library of Congress, 22; Corbis, 9, 18, 21; Frederick Dielman/Library of
Congress, 27; Howard Pyle/Bettmann/Corbis, 5; Hulton-Deutsch Collection/Corbis, 8; North
Wind Picture Archives, 7, 10, 11, 12, 14, 16, 23; William Henry Shelton/Corbis, 19

LIBRARY OF CONGRESS CATALOGING-IN-PUBLICATION DATA

Meadows, James, 1969–

  Slavery : the struggle for freedom / by James Meadows.

      p. cm. — (Journey to freedom)

  Includes bibliographical references and index.

  ISBN 978-1-60253-134-5 (library bound : alk. paper)

  1. Slavery—United States—History—Juvenile literature. 2. Slavery—America—History—Juvenile literature. 3. Slaves—United States—Social conditions—Juvenile literature. 4. Slaves—America—Social conditions—Juvenile literature. 5. African Americans—History—To 1863—Juvenile
literature. 6. Blacks—America—History—Juvenile literature. I. Title.

  E441.M48 2009

  306.3'62'0973—dc22

                              2008031938

CONTENTS

American settlers look on as slaves captured in Africa arrive in Jamestown in 1619.

Chapter One

THE BEGINNING

he first slave ships set sail from Europe around 1450, more than 500 years ago. They sailed to Africa from the country of Portugal. At the time, Portugal was one of the wealthiest, most powerful nations in Europe. Even so, it did not have enough farm workers. Portuguese slave traders captured Africans and brought them back to Europe.

Soon, other Europeans, as well as Arab slave traders from North Africa, became active in the slave trade. They took people from central Africa to sell not only in Europe but also in Eastern lands such as Arabia and India. Beginning in 1619, slave traders shipped Africans across the Atlantic Ocean to the New World. Once there, the enslaved

A different type of slavery existed in Africa before the Europeans entered the slave trade. When African tribes were at war, captured soldiers often became slaves. These captives sometimes became part of their new culture rather than remaining slaves. They often married into the new tribe. Sometimes slaves even rose to positions of leadership and power.

Africans were sold like livestock. They were forced to work on farms, clean houses, or do anything else their masters wanted. They worked long hours for no pay. If they refused to work, they could be beaten or killed.

European slave traders made a huge profit by selling human beings into **bondage**. The slave ships sailed south from Europe toward West Africa. Some Africans were blacksmiths or miners. Others were farmers, priests, and politicians. They were leaders and warriors, parents and children. Millions of African people were torn from their families, their homes, their land, and their goods to be sold as property.

Although slavery ended almost 150 years ago, learning about it today helps us understand the **racism** and **prejudice** that still exist. We can be inspired by the courage of those who endured slavery and those who fought to end it. We can better appreciate the United States' struggle to hold true to its values of freedom and equality.

Africa is the second largest continent on Earth. It features two of the world's largest deserts, endless plains, and miles of rain forest. Africa's people are as diverse as their land. They speak hundreds of different languages. Tribes and clans often have very different religious traditions and customs. When slave traders first arrived, Africans had a difficult time banding together to fight back because their languages and customs often were so different.

Slaves captured in Africa march to the coast to be sold into slavery.

Once captured, most Africans spent their entire lives in bondage.

When European slave traders captured new slaves in Africa, other Africans often helped them. Some African clans helped the slave traders capture their enemies. Europeans also bribed Africans with cloth, guns, and other forms of wealth. Later, Africans helped the slave traders to avoid being sold into slavery themselves.

Once captured, most Africans remained slaves their entire lives. Their children were born into slavery as well. Soon after slavery reached North America, lawmakers made it illegal for slaves to learn to read. Although many enslaved Africans had lifelong partners and families, they could not legally marry.

At the time, most Europeans believed that Africans were savages who lacked intelligence and needed whites to guide them. This was how the Europeans justified slavery. History tells a different story about African cultures. Many Africans lived in large, wealthy kingdoms such as Ghana, Mali, and Songhai.

Unfortunately, the slave trade changed the entire region. European slave traders captured thousands of Africa's strongest, most capable people. The captives were shipped to the other side of the world, year after year, for hundreds of years.

Why did Europeans create such a brutal trade? In the 1490s and early 1500s, European explorers sailed across the Atlantic looking for a faster, cheaper way to the Asian lands of India and China. Instead, the explorers found the continents known today as North and South America.

Europeans claimed the vast lands of this New World, which was already home to millions of Native Americans. As the Europeans took the land from the Native Americans, they needed cheap labor to grow crops, build towns, and provide goods and services.

Slave masters examine an African brought to a slave market near Africa's Kambia River. This image is a reproduction of a painting done by Francois Biard in 1840.

Colonists force a Native American into slavery in the 1600s.

First, they tried enslaving Native Americans. However, many Native Americans were hunters more than farmers. They were not well suited to the work. A vast number died from **inhumane** treatment or from diseases the Europeans brought with them. Those who survived knew the land well enough to escape, and sometimes they could fight back.

When enslaving Native Americans proved unsuccessful, the Europeans brought in African slaves. Many of the new slaves had been farmers in Africa and were used to the work. They already had been exposed to many of the diseases the Europeans brought from the Old World. And African slaves were less likely to escape because they did not know the lands of their new home. They had nowhere to go.

Chapter Two

SLAVERY IN NORTH AMERICA

fricans captured inland in Africa were sometimes forced to march hundreds of miles to the coast. During this exhausting journey, they were tied at the hands and neck. They marched all day and long into the evening, stopping only for a little food and water. Those who could not keep up were beaten or left to die.

Once the captives reached the coast, they were loaded onto slave ships. The more slaves each ship carried, the more money the slave traders made. The voyage across the Atlantic Ocean to North America, often called the Middle Passage, was long and cruel. The captives were chained to the deck

Slavery expanded when Eli Whitney invented the cotton gin in 1793. The cotton gin meant cotton could be processed much more quickly. More slaves were needed to keep up with the demand.

for days at a time. They were packed in shoulder to shoulder and hip to hip. Forced to lie in their own waste and vomit, they fell victim to deadly diseases such as smallpox. Due to the awful conditions, one-third of the captives never survived the trip. Some killed themselves by jumping overboard to escape the misery.

The first enslaved Africans landed in North America in 1619. These first Africans were indentured servants. This meant that they worked for seven to ten years before being freed. These freed slaves and their families were among the free blacks living in the North and the South during later years of slavery. But the opportunity for earning freedom did not last long. Wealthy landowners soon saw that they could make more money by keeping the Africans enslaved for life. New laws made it more difficult to free blacks and increased the punishment for slaves who ran away.

Before the North American colonies declared and won their independence from England in the late 1770s, slavery existed in every colony. Enslaved blacks worked in shops in the North and on **plantations** in the South. After the

Slaves pick cotton on a plantation.

This illustration shows men in a slave market around 1850. The slaves were held in chains before being sold to new owners.

Revolutionary War, some states in the North **abolished** slavery. People reasoned that to truly believe in freedom, they could not allow slavery to exist in their states. Many people also saw that slave labor, especially in the cities, was not much cheaper than hiring workers.

The majority of the people in the South had a different view. They refused to give up slavery. The disagreement between the North and the South almost split the new nation in two. Northerners avoided a break by allowing slavery into the **Constitution**. Although the Constitution does not mention slaves directly, it recognizes them indirectly by saying that only

Slavery continued even after Thomas Jefferson wrote the Declaration of Independence in 1776. It stated that "all men are created equal." Both Jefferson and George Washington owned slaves, despite the fact that each of them had mixed feelings about slavery.

three-fifths of non-free persons would be included in the population count. More than 70 years later, the disagreement that led to this compromise helped spark the nation's Civil War.

Abolishing slavery in parts of the North created large populations of free blacks in those states. Free blacks did not have the same rights as whites, but they had more rights than slaves. Many free blacks in the North used their freedom to help slaves escape.

Slaves are shown using Eli Whitney's cotton gin.

A slave is sold on the auction block after arriving in the American colonies.

Chapter Three

A SLAVE'S LIFE

or many blacks, life in the New World began on the auction block. The auction block was a place, often in the center of town, where cows, horses, and slaves were bought and sold. Most slave owners were looking for slaves who were strong. These slaves could work hard for long hours, plowing the land and harvesting crops such as corn, tobacco, and cotton. The buyers looked over the naked and chained new arrivals. They checked their teeth as if the slaves were horses. To the slave owners, blacks were less than human. They were little more than animals bought to perform certain tasks.

Many slave owners used cruelty to force their slaves to work. Slaves could be whipped for not

House slaves often had better living conditions and shorter working hours than field hands. Some slave owners eventually freed their house servants.

working quickly enough, for not getting out to the fields by dawn, or for almost anything else. Masters of larger farms often hired an **overseer** to ensure the slaves worked hard, did not rebel, and did not run away. Many overseers were known for being exceptionally cruel.

Frederick Douglass, an **abolitionist** and **fugitive** slave, described his overseer: "Mr. Severe was rightly named; he was a cruel man. I have seen him whip a woman, causing the blood to run half an hour at a time; and this too, in the midst of her crying children pleading for their mother's release."

The whips used for punishment were often several feet long and made of stiff cowhide. A single stroke of the whip could draw blood. Several strokes could make a person unconscious from the pain or cause death.

A slave mother and daughter are sold on the auction block. Often, family members were separated.

Slave owners often separated families. Children were taken from their parents. Husbands could be sold away from their wives, and brothers and sisters could be separated. Douglass wrote, "I never saw my mother, to know her as such, more than four or five times in my life. . . . She died when I was about seven years old, on one of my master's farms, near Lee's Mill. I was not allowed to be present during her illness, at her death, or burial. She was gone long before I knew anything about it."

It was illegal to teach a slave to read. Slave owners sometimes disobeyed this law, but most enslaved blacks were not given the chance to learn. Slave owners wanted to keep the slaves completely dependent on their masters. How far could an escaped slave run without knowing how to read? Enslaved children without parents were dependent on their white masters, no matter how cruel they were. Dependent slaves were less likely to run away or kill their masters.

While slaves were housed and fed, they rarely had enough to eat—perhaps a pint (.47 l) of rice or grain and less than a pound (.45 kg) of meat for an entire week. Often the food was rotten. Slaves were sheltered in structures that looked more like horse barns than houses. The rough boards did not keep the wind out or the heat in. Instead of beds, the slaves slept on narrow boards or a dirt floor. Nothing in the slaves' lives belonged to them—not their clothes, their homes, their children, their work, or even their bodies. Slave owners

Pregnant slaves worked until they gave birth, then were given a month of rest. After that, they carried their babies on their backs while working. Children were expected to start working at age five.

Most slaves knew little about their personal history. As Frederick Douglass wrote, "By far the larger part of the slaves know as little of their ages as horses know of theirs, and it is the wish of most masters within my knowledge to keep their slaves thus ignorant."

regularly took advantage of their female slaves because no laws protected the women from rape.

Even when not working, enslaved blacks had little freedom. They were not allowed to leave the plantation without permission from the master. They could not meet in groups, even to talk about the weather. They could not buy or sell goods or hire themselves out to do a job. They were not allowed to have guns. They could not beat drums. Almost any white person could whip or beat an enslaved black for practically any reason. Slaves had no legal protection from any white person on or off the master's farm.

Slaves experienced terrible conditions when they were brought across the Atlantic. Many lawmakers were aware of this. In 1808, the U.S. government made it illegal to bring slaves into the country, but the law did not stop people from buying and selling slaves who were already here. And **smugglers** still brought slaves over from Africa illegally, although the new law did reduce the number.

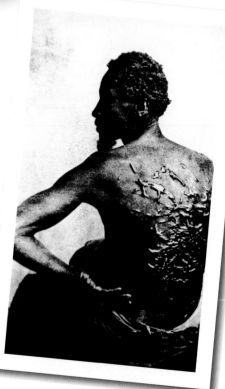

This slave's back was scarred after he was whipped by his master.

Nat Turner is discovered by a slave hunter. Turner led a slave uprising in 1831.

Chapter Four

RESISTANCE

any slave owners lived in fear that their slaves would rebel or fight back. Newspapers regularly reported instances of slaves poisoning or stabbing their owners. Some slaves injured themselves so they could not work. Others killed themselves to end a lifetime of slavery. Thousands of enslaved blacks ran away, costing their owners a great deal of money.

Other slaves organized in groups to rise up against their masters. Gabriel Prosser led a famous **revolt** in 1800. More than 1,000 Virginia blacks, led by Prosser, armed themselves and marched on Richmond. The revolt fell apart after two slaves reported the plan to whites.

The governor of Virginia sent troops to crush the uprising. Prosser and other leaders were captured and executed.

Denmark Vesey led a similar revolt in Charlestown, South Carolina, in 1822. Vesey had bought his freedom more than 20 years earlier. For many years, he had gathered weapons and supporters with the aim of ending slavery in the region. An estimated 9,000 slaves were involved in the plot, but word reached the local authorities. Before Vesey's revolt could begin, 139 blacks were arrested. Forty-seven blacks were executed. Four whites went to prison for helping with the revolt.

Nat Turner, a slave and a preacher, led the most effective slave revolt in the United States. In 1831, Turner and other blacks grouped together and killed approximately 60 whites in Southampton, Virginia. State and federal troops eventually stopped Turner's small army. Turner escaped but was later captured and executed. His revolt encouraged many blacks to fight for their freedom. It also horrified many whites because it destroyed their belief that blacks were happy to be enslaved.

Every year, thousands of slaves ran away to freedom. Some escaped alone, but many others had help from the **Underground Railroad**. The Underground Railroad was not an actual railroad, but a group of people in both the North and the South who helped blacks escape slavery. They gave the runaways food and shelter during the long journey north. Some "conductors" on

This portrait of Harriet Tubman is thought to have been taken in the 1860s. After escaping slavery, Tubman became a conductor on the Underground Railroad.

Many women took a special interest in abolishing slavery. Women such as Sojourner Truth, Lucretia Mott, and Lydia Marie Child believed a nation that enslaved blacks would never fully respect the rights of women.

the Underground Railroad went with the runaways, directing them to safety. The most famous conductor was Harriet Tubman. She escaped slavery herself as a young woman but returned to the South many times to help other slaves escape.

Escaping slavery was not easy. The runaways had to travel hundreds of miles on foot. They moved by night and hid by day, often disguising themselves. Most importantly, they had to avoid patrols and bounty hunters. Patrols were groups of armed whites who regularly traveled an area, looking for runaway blacks. Bounty hunters chased and caught runaways to collect a reward for their return.

Slaves escape on foot and on horseback with the help of the Underground Railroad.

THE LIBERATOR.

HORSE MARKET

SLAVES, HORSES & OTHER CAT-TLE TO BE SOLD AT 12 oc.

[NO. 22

WILLIAM LLOYD GARRISON AND ISAAC KNAPP, PUBLISHERS. [SATURDAY, MAY 28, 1831.

VOL. I.]

OUR COUNTRY IS THE WORLD—OUR COUNTRYMEN ARE MANKIND.

BOSTON, MASSACHUSETTS.]

The *Liberator*, published by William Lloyd Garrison, was one of several antislavery newspapers that sprang up in the North.

Chapter Five

SLAVERY'S END

y the 1830s, enslaved blacks had become a major workforce. In many parts of the South, black slaves far outnumbered white people. As slavery grew, so did opposition to it. How could a nation founded on "life, liberty, and the pursuit of happiness" deny even the most basic freedoms to millions of human beings?

Northerners, both black and white, spoke out more and more against slavery. People who opposed slavery called themselves abolitionists because they wanted to abolish, or end, slavery.

Several antislavery newspapers sprang up in the North. The most famous was called the *Liberator*. It appeared in January of 1831. The editor, a

Frederick Douglass, a well-known abolitionist, spoke out against slavery in his speeches and writings.

In 1845, Frederick Douglass published his own story, Narrative of the Life of Frederick Douglass, An American Slave. The book became a best-seller and now is considered an American classic.

white man named William Lloyd Garrison, became one of the nation's most outspoken critics of slavery. Two years before the *Liberator* first appeared, a free black man named David Walker printed a powerful essay. He declared that black people had the right to resist slavery—with force, if necessary. His powerful words terrified many whites and challenged blacks to win their freedom.

Dozens of abolitionists formed groups, wrote letters to the government, and gave lectures condemning slavery. Perhaps the greatest among them was Frederick Douglass. While enslaved in the South, Douglass learned to read. He escaped slavery as a young man and became the nation's most forceful antislavery speaker and writer. Douglass eventually created his own antislavery newspaper called the *North Star*. He chose the name because runaway slaves often used the North Star to guide them at night.

Douglass and other abolitionists convinced many Northerners to oppose slavery. As antislavery beliefs grew, the nation became more and more divided.

In the mid-1800s, the United States was still expanding. Most Southerners wanted slavery to be allowed in the new territories. Most Northerners did not. Disagreement in the territories became so strong that citizens in the North and South began to fight one another.

Disagreement was serious in the U.S. Congress as well. Representatives and senators from the South threatened to withdraw their states from the **Union** if they were not allowed to bring slavery into the new territories. They believed that individual states should be able to decide whether or not slavery should be allowed. Northerners believed the national government should decide. The United States faced a major crisis. If Southern states left the Union, or **seceded**, the government would have to use force to keep the nation united.

The disagreement between the North and South helped drive the United States toward a civil war. Abraham Lincoln was elected president in 1860. Much of the South believed that Lincoln was an abolitionist who wanted to destroy slavery. Several Southern states decided to secede and form their own country. When Southern troops attacked a U.S. fort on April 12, 1861, Union troops fought back. The U.S. Civil War had begun.

At the start of the war, slavery was not the main issue for the federal government. President Lincoln knew that many Northerners would not fight a war to free slaves, but they would fight to preserve the Union. Southerners said they were fighting for individual states' rights. Even so, blacks knew that the war could decide the future of slavery.

Abraham Lincoln led the nation as it struggled with the issue of slavery.

General Robert E. Lee surrendered his Southern army to General Ulysses S. Grant on April 9, 1865. The North won the war, but President Lincoln did not live to see the end of slavery. Lincoln was assassinated on April 14, 1865, before the Thirteenth Amendment became law.

At first, the Union army turned away black volunteers. Even though many Northerners opposed slavery, they still had racist beliefs. But after Union troops lost battle after battle to the South, the North decided to allow blacks to join the Union army. Blacks knew that this was their time to fight for freedom. Thousands of free blacks joined the army, and thousands more escaped slavery to join as well.

Black troops were not treated as equals. They received lower pay and poor equipment. At first, they were not even allowed to fight in battles. But the South kept beating the North in battles, and the Union army needed more troops. Eventually, the Union army treated its black troops better.

Although the U.S. Civil War was fought for a number of reasons, it finally led to the end of slavery. In January of 1863, President Lincoln issued the Emancipation Proclamation, which freed slaves in all rebel states. Lincoln did not have the power to enforce the order at that time, but the act itself helped the North in its fight.

Black troops fought bravely in many battles, helping the North win the Civil War. They fought to keep the nation together, but they also fought for freedom—for themselves and for others. People knew that if the South won the war, slavery would continue. When the North won in 1865, the end of slavery was in sight.

Slavery did not end right away, however. The U.S. Congress had to pass **amendments** to the Constitution to put an end to slavery for good. In 1865, the Thirteenth Amendment made slavery illegal. In 1868, the Fourteenth Amendment made all former slaves citizens, like anyone else born in the United States. The Fifteenth Amendment gave black men the right to vote in 1870. (Women of all races did not win the right to vote in the United States until 1920, with the passing of the Nineteenth Amendment.)

The end of slavery did not mean the end of racism. The government did not always enforce these new amendments to the Constitution. The end of slavery was the beginning of another long journey—the struggle to bring equal treatment to all people. That journey continues today.

Slavery was a terrible institution that destroyed the lives of many people. Millions of people endured slavery or fought to end it. Learning about their struggles can help us appreciate the value of freedom.

Freed slaves celebrate the abolition of slavery.

TIME LINE

1501
Europeans begin transporting enslaved Africans to the Western Hemisphere to replace Native American slaves.

1619
The first enslaved Africans land in North America at the settlement of Jamestown.

1776
The United States declares its independence from England. Thomas Jefferson writes in the Declaration of Independence that "all men are created equal."

1787
The U.S. Constitution allows slavery to exist in the new nation.

1800
Gabriel Prosser leads a large but unsuccessful slave revolt in Virginia.

1808
A new law makes it illegal to bring slaves to the United States from Africa.

1822
Denmark Vesey, a free black man, plots a large slave revolt in South Carolina. Whites discover the plot, and the revolt never takes place.

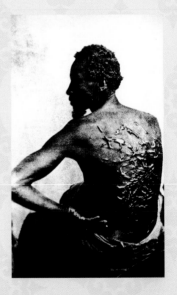

1831

William Lloyd Garrison, a white abolitionist, founds an antislavery newspaper called the *Liberator*.

1831

Nat Turner leads a Virginia slave rebellion in which about 60 whites are killed. Turner and his men are eventually captured and executed.

1847

Frederick Douglass, a black abolitionist and fugitive slave, starts an antislavery newspaper called the *North Star*.

1860

Abraham Lincoln is elected president of the United States. Southerners believe he is an abolitionist who will end slavery.

1861

Many Southern states secede from the United States. This action leads to the U.S. Civil War, which begins on April 12.

1863

Abraham Lincoln issues the Emancipation Proclamation.

1865

The North defeats the South in the Civil War.

1865

The Thirteenth Amendment to the U.S. Constitution declares slavery to be illegal.

1868

The Fourteenth Amendment to the Constitution grants full citizenship to all former slaves.

1870

The Fifteenth Amendment guarantees black men the right to vote.

GLOSSARY

abolished
*(uh-**bol**-ishd)*
Abolished means putting an end to something officially. In the United States, slavery was finally abolished after the end of the Civil War, with the passage of the Thirteenth Amendment.

abolitionist
*(ab-uh-**lish**-uh-nist)*
An abolitionist was someone who worked to abolish slavery before the Civil War. Frederick Douglass was a famous abolitionist.

amendments
*(uh-**mend**-munts)*
Amendments are changes that are made to a law or legal document. Congress had to pass amendments to the Constitution to end slavery.

bondage
*(**bon**-dij)*
People who are kept in bondage are held against their will. Enslaved Africans were held in bondage.

Constitution
*(kon-stuh-**too**-shun)*
The Constitution is the written document containing the principles by which the United States is governed. The Constitution had to be amended to outlaw slavery.

fugitive
*(**fyoo**-juh-tiv)*
Someone who is running away, especially from the law, is a fugitive. A runaway slave was a fugitive.

inhumane
*(in-hyoo-**mayn**)*
Inhumane means cruel and brutal. Treatment of slaves was often inhumane.

overseer
*(**oh**-vur-see-ur)*
An overseer is a person who supervises others as they work. On plantations, an overseer supervised the slaves.

plantations
*(plan-**tay**-shuns)*
Plantations are large farms, often in the South. Many slaves were forced to work on plantations.

prejudice
*(**prej**-uh-diss)*
Prejudice means a negative feeling or opinion about someone without just cause. Even after slavery ended, prejudice about race continued.

racism
*(**ray**-sih-zum)*
The belief that one race is superior to another is called racism. Racism remained a problem even after slavery had ended.

revolt
*(ri-**volt**)*
A revolt is a rebellion against a government or an authority. Nat Turner led a famous slave revolt.

secede
*(sih-**seed**)*
To secede is to formally withdraw from an organization, often to form another organization. At the start of the U.S. Civil War, Southern states decided to secede from the United States to form their own nation.

smugglers
*(**smug**-lerz)*
Smugglers are people who bring goods into a country illegally. Bringing slaves into the United States eventually became illegal, but smugglers still brought them in.

Underground Railroad
*(**un**-der-grownd **rayl**-rohd)*
The Underground Railroad was a group of people who helped blacks escape slavery before the U.S. Civil War. Many people worked hard to make the Underground Railroad a success.

Union
*(**yoon**-yuhn)*
Union is another way of referring to the United States of America. The Union won the U.S. Civil War.

Further Information

Books

Douglass, Frederick. *Narrative of the Life of Frederick Douglass, an American Slave*. New York: Barnes & Noble Classics, 2005.

Jordan, Anne Devereaux. *Slavery and Resistance: The Drama of African-American History*. New York: Benchmark Books, 2006.

Kallen, Stuart A. *A History of Free Blacks in America*. Farmington Hills, MI: Lucent Books, 2005.

Kamma, Anne. *If You Lived When There Was Slavery in America*. New York: Scholastic, 2004.

Landau, Elaine. *The Abolitionist Movement*. New York: Scholastic, 2004.

Sirimarco, Elizabeth. *The Time of Slavery*. Tarrytown, NY: Marshall Cavendish, 2006.

Videos

Slave Catchers, Slave Resisters. A&E Home Video, 2005.

Slavery and the Making of America. Ambrose, 2005.

Web Sites

Visit our Web page for links about slavery and the struggle for freedom:

http://www.childsworld.com/links

NOTE TO PARENTS, TEACHERS, AND LIBRARIANS: We routinely verify our Web links to make sure they are safe, active sites—so encourage your readers to check them out!

INDEX